LOVE HOUND

LOVE HOUND

Oliver Welden

1968 Luis Tello National Poetry Award
Society of Chilean Writers
2007 New York Book Festival
Best Book of Poetry Award
2007 Benjamin Franklin Awards
Honorable Mention

translated from the Spanish and with an introduction by
Dave Oliphant

HOST PUBLICATIONS
AUSTIN, TX

Host Publications, Inc. 1000 East 7ᵗʰ, Suite 201, Austin, TX 78702

Layout and Design:	Joe Bratcher & Anand Ramaswamy
Cover & book images:	Guillermo Deisler (1940-1995)
Cover Design:	Anand Ramaswamy
Back Cover Photo:	Alicia Galaz (1927-2003)
	Oliver Welden in 1970, the year of publication
	of *Love Hound* in its original Spanish version.

Library of Congress Catalog Number: 2006927027
ISBN 10: 0-924047-31-3
ISBN 13: 978-0-9240-4731-2

First Edition

TABLE OF CONTENTS

I
Cadáver con fruta
Corpse With Fruit

II
De un tiempo a estas partes
For a While Now

III
La manzana del gusano
The Worm's Apple

INTRODUCTION

In February 1973, three young, aspiring poets, with only a few pesos in their pockets and rolled, twine-tied blankets on their backs, began to hitchhike from Santiago, the capital of Chile in the middle of this 3,000-mile-long country, north toward Arica, a city almost on the border with Peru. The trio would catch rides with truck drivers delivering foodstuffs and machine parts to towns dotting the second worst desert in the world, Chile's extensive Atacama. Their reason for making this 1500-mile trip in worn-out shoes, and at the mercy of the heat by day and the chill by night, was to find the poet Oliver Welden, author of *Perro del amor* (*Love Hound*), a book whose title the young men considered iconoclastic and entirely new to Chilean letters. Through their pilgrimage to Arica they would render homage to Welden, who, in 1968, at the age of twenty-two, had won for his manuscript of *Perro del amor* the prestigious national prize, "Luis Tello," awarded by the Chilean Society of Writers. Subsequently, in 1970, *Perro del amor* was published in a beautifully designed edition illustrated by the Chilean artist Guillermo Deisler. Thirty-two years from the time of that journey to Arica, Javier Campos, one of the three young poets, recalled his trek to Arica and the lasting impact of the twenty-three poems that comprise Welden's modest volume. More than three decades after its original appearance, Welden's book has still not been forgotten, despite the fact, as Campos reports, that no copy of *Perro del amor* is held by the National Library nor by any other library in Chile.

My own awareness of this recently "rediscovered" book dates from 1971. In February of that year, I read in the final issue of the important magazine *Mundo Nuevo*, published in Paris, a mini-anthology introduced and compiled by Oliver Welden and his poet-wife Alicia Galaz Vivar, based on the work of poets that they were then publishing from the city of Arica in their seminal magazine *Tebaida*. That summer my wife María Isabel and I visited her native Chile, and from Santiago I made contact with Oliver and Alicia. Through the patronage of the U.S. Embassy and the University of Chile in Arica, we were able to fly to the country's northern-most city, where we would meet the two poets and Oliver would present me with an inscribed copy of his *Perro del amor*. The next year, in 1972, six of the poems from Oliver's book would appear in an anthology of Chilean poetry that I selected and translated for *Road Apple Review* of Oshkosh, Wisconsin. American poet Robert Bly, who saw that spring number of the Wisconsin magazine, wrote to the editors to thank them for bringing the Chilean poets to his attention, and in his letter, he singled out the poetry of Oliver Welden as his favorite among the work of the twenty-two poets represented in that special *Road Apple* issue.

At the time of the first appearance of *Perro del amor* in 1970, Welden's book was widely reviewed in Chile, in particular by such major critics as Ignacio Valente, Hernán del Solar, and Hernán Loyola, as well as by a number of prominent poets, including Jorge Teillier, Omar Lara, Waldo Rojas, Andrés Sabella, Ariel Santibáñez, and Floridor Pérez. The reviews uniformly celebrated Welden's fresh, pared down, but penetrating language. In Chile's main newspaper, *El Mercurio*, Ignacio Valente commented that Welden's poems are both objective and intense in communicating a sense of disillusion with life as it is so often lived. This critic noted that the poet picks at his own feelings without either pleasure or compassion. Also in *El Mercurio*, Hernán del Solar pointed out that the poet positions himself midway between rebelliousness and a submission tickled by sarcasm, that he is a poet of a vital expression, not in terms of exalting or diminishing his subjects but rather of allowing his language to present an attitude perfectly natural in the face of an unnatural, monotonous, mechanical existence. In the leftist newspaper, *El Siglo*, Hernán Loyola characterized *Perro del amor* as filling with lyric potency the seemingly lightest and most trivial anecdotes. The critic also summarized the three sections of the book as presenting, first, a tragic dimension in terms of solitude, suicide, and murder; second, the atmosphere within a degraded family; and third, through a spare and economic treatment, the powerful emotional density of the erotic. For his part, Jorge Teillier observed in *¡Puro Chile!* that Welden's "black" poetry reflects an adolescent's desperate search for himself, expressed through a ruthless diction concise as any epitaph.

On September 11, 1973, a military coup overthrew the democratically elected government of Socialist President Salvador Allende, and Chile's sympathetic poets were forced into exile or chose to leave rather than live under a military dictatorship. Oliver and Alicia left Chile for the United States and were never to return to their country, unlike most all the poets who eventually went back following the end of the Pinochet regime. Settling in Alabama, the couple continued to write, with Oliver completing three poetry manuscripts, but he never published any of his poems until four appeared in 2005 in the magazine *Trilce*, edited by Omar Lara, who declared Welden "one of the most outstanding poets of the Generation of 1960."

Novelist Roberto Bolaño notes in an interview that appeared in *El Mercurio* on October 25, 2003, "I remember Oliver Welden, of whom nowadays in Chile no one has the least notion of his name. He was a poet of Arica and quite good, from the little it was possible to read by him." Nevertheless, by 2005, references to Welden began to crop up in publications not alone in Chile but elsewhere. From Panama, Rolando Gabrielli wrote for a periodical in Buenos Aires to wonder "what has become of the poet Oliver

Welden who one spring afternoon traveled to the United States
. . . and disappeared among the diaspora . . . . I have in my hands
Perro del amor and I read in it a poetry that nests in my memory. It
regales us with good poems and I place it on the table more than
three decades afterwards, because it is never late when poetry lets
us experience new things no matter how old it may be."
Throughout Chile various voices recalled the book and its author
with both nostalgia and regret. From the South of Chile, Virginia
Vidal wrote that "the name Oliver Welden is inevitably linked to
his book *Perro del amor*," and from La Serena, Arturo Volantines
pronounced *Perro del amor* an "important book that is already part
of the heritage of Chilean literature," holding up its author as "a
notable example of the artist, in his ethics of poetry and in his
social significance," lamenting at the same time that "undoubtedly
exile did enormous damage in dispersing his generation." From
Valparaíso, Carlos Amador Marchant asked of his readers, "Permit
me to bring back to the present day the name Oliver Welden . . .
who has been silenced during three decades. Can one find his
books *Anhista* and *Perro del amor* in some out of the way place in
Chile's long geography? Impossible, there aren't any and how such
texts are missed."

To make Oliver Welden's memorable, prize-winning book
available, both to Chilean and to English readers here and abroad,
Host Publications proudly offers *Perro del amor* in this bilingual
edition, along with some of the woodcuts by Guillermo Deisler
that originally graced the 1970 publication. That Welden's poetry
has survived the test of time is amply demonstrated by the many
tributes to his thin collection of twenty-three poems, not only on
its first appearance but thirty-five years later. The enduring interest
in the poet's work is also attested to by the fact that two of his
previously unpublished books, *Oscura palabra* and *Fábulas ocultas*,
will appear this year from presses in Chile. To provide but one

example of the poet's writing from the years that he and Alicia spent separated from their native Chile, I conclude with a translation of Oliver's "Autumn in Alabama," with its epigraph from a poem by his companion in life and poetry who departed this world in 2003.

Autumn in Alabama

And I find myself on an afternoon of shadows
while the rain runs off, once again the rain,
and it moves away with a noise of bones.
                                    – Alicia Galaz Vivar
                        from "The Exile That Never Leaves Me"

When to us all that exists is alien
and decidedly doesn't belong to us,
our country even, strange and distant,
like an old umbrella closed in memory,
you cling to love as a cripple to his crutch
and begin to write
Autumn in Alabama
in order to tell yourself, oh how profoundly:
all that exists is alien to us
and, don't you know? decidedly doesn't belong to us.
Then the leaves fall as the leaves fall
in all the autumns of the earth.

Ven, perro, con tus palabras.

Para descubrirnos y nombrarnos después en los años
como algo propio que conserva su sabiduría
-para Alicia compañera y nuestros terribles fantasmas-
abro aquí este viejo maletín del amor.

Quédate, perro, con tus palabras.

Come, hound, with your words.

For discovering and naming us in after years
as something appropriate for preserving their sense
-for my companion Alicia and our terrible phantoms-
I open this old satchel of love.

Stay, hound, with your words.

La grandeza progresa en el mundo,
a medida que la intimidad se profundiza.

Bachelard

Greatness progresses in the world,
according to the deepening of intimacy.

Bachelard

PERRO DEL AMOR

LOVE HOUND

I

Cadáver con fruta

I

Corpse With Fruit

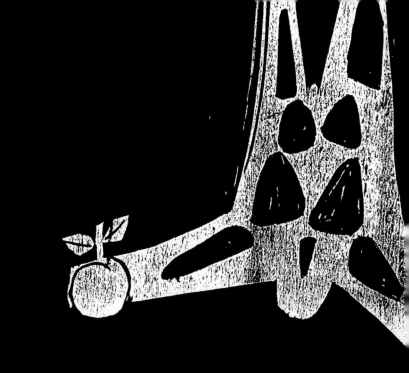

Credenciales

Fulano de Tal, de infeliz memoria,
acogido al desencanto y criado en la impostura,
revela aquí su amargura
y expone, paso a paso, su conducta perentoria,
mientras se sube a la silla
y al cuello se ajusta la soga.

En el piso, señor juez, la carta justificatoria,
otra a su esposa, otra a su madre
y en alguna parte de la casa
el teléfono que llama, brevemente,
demasiado tarde.

Credentials

What's-his-name, of unhappy memory,
inmate of disillusionment and raised on falsehood,
reveals here his bitterness
and exposes, step by step, his decisive conduct
as he climbs on the chair
and pulls the rope knot tight.
On the floor, your Honor, the justifying note,
another to his wife, another to his mother
and in some part of the house
the telephone that rings, briefly,
belatedly.

Advertencia

Érase un hombre solo,
demasiado solo;
cuando sentado en el baño
dejaba correr el agua
para escuchar su sonido;
en su oficina de correos dialogaba
con las cartas y en sueños
visitaba a los destinatarios. Falleció
la primavera recién pasada:
al cajón le ajustaron las manillas por dentro
para que esa mañana
se condujera solo al cementerio.

Warning

He was a loner,
too much so;
when seated in the bathtub
he let the water run
to hear its sound;
in his postal office he conversed
with the letters and in dreams
visited the addressees. He died
just this past spring:
they adjusted the coffin handles from the inside
so that that morning
he could cart himself to the graveyard.

Axioma vital

Las moscas ocultan el corazón
porque el corazón es una magnífica bosta.

Vital Axiom

Flies darken the heart
for the heart's a magnificent turd.

Sobremesa

La cocina de la pensión está inmóvil
los platos despedazados en el lavaplatos
y las ollas apiladas.
En el centro mismo con los pies
a la altura de la ampolleta
la alpargata oscilando amarrada a un tobillo
puesto fin ya a sus días oscuros
la mama de la casa cuelga fija.
Abajo entre la silla volcada
la tetera se derrama lentamente.

After Eating

The kitchen in the boarding house is still
the chipped plates in the sink
and the pots piled high.
In the very middle with feet
at the height of the light bulb
the rope-soled shoe tied to an ankle oscillating
putting an end now to her dark days
the nanny of the house hangs unmoving.
Below within the overturned chair
the kettle slowly dribbles.

Vaivenes

Puede que haya pasado demasiado tiempo,
más que el necesario,
pero estimo necesario esperar todavía
el amaino de la resaca
para amarrar mi cuerpo
a la roca semisumergida,
cerrar los ojos y abrir la boca
y esperar, nuevamente,
a que suba del todo la marea.

Fluctuations

It may be that too much time has passed,
more than enough,
but I figure it's necessary to keep waiting
for the tide to go out
in order to tie my body
to the half-submerged rock,
to close my eyes and open my mouth
and wait, once more,
for the surf to rise.

La fiesta

Oigo morir. Se desmorona mi gesto.
Voy envejeciendo durante la noche con una mano
en la boca. Mi vómito se arrastra remando
cama abajo. Estoy desnudo esperando. Oigo morir.
La pieza clavada en el silencio parpadea. Me escondo.
Pero qué mal te escondes hijo de puta.

The Party

I hear dying. My face is disintegrating.
I go on growing old in the night with a hand
in my mouth. My vomit trails off the bed
paddling down. I'm naked waiting. I hear dying.
The room nailed in the silence blinks. I hide myself.
But how poorly you conceal yourself you son of a bitch.

El superhombre

De este lado siempre estamos vivos,
con diarreas ocasionales, suaves úlceras abiertas,
la arterioesclerosis hasta en los testículos,
con todo siempre estamos vivos, machacando la dulce
insistencia de amanecer cada día,
sentados en la cama escuchando el corazón.
Acabo perdiendo una hora
eliminando el temblor de los párpados, la mejilla.
–Tú sabes tratarme, me digo.
Con el chal en las espaldas echo correr la silla
de ruedas hacia el sol de la terraza.

Superman

On this side we are always alive,
with occasional diarrhea, soft open ulcers,
arteriosclerosis even in the testicles,
with all this still alive, chewing the sweet
insistence of awaking each day,
sitting in bed listening to the heart.
I've just lost an hour
eliminating the trembling of eyelids, the cheek.
–You know how to take care of me, I tell myself.
With the shawl on my shoulders I start the wheelchair
rolling toward sun out on the terrace.

II

De un tiempo a estas partes

II

For a While Now

Fotografía

Lo que nunca nadie fue en mi familia
y todo lo que rechazaron
el obrero el sastre el profesor primario
lo tengo aquí en mí protegido
con la fuerza esa que tuvo mi padre
la noche que golpeó a mi madre
embarazada de mi hermana menor.

Photograph

What no one in my family ever was
and all that they rejected
the worker the tailor the grade school teacher
I hold here in my protection
with the same force my father used
the night he beat my mother
pregnant with my younger sister.

Statu quo

Vuelve a mí la terrible angustia
de la infancia, esa timidez
conocida, y es preciso que no me mueva
para no caer,
como mi padre y mi madre,
como tanto ídolo roto de esos años.

Status Quo

The terrible anguish of my youth
returns to me, that familiar
timidity, and it's necessary that I not move
so as not to fall,
as did my father and my mother,
as did from those years many a broken idol.

Reincidencia

Hubo en mi casa espectáculos poco afortunados.
Mi abuelo cumplía entonces 18 años
y a la mesa llegaba un padrastro que ocupaba
la cabecera; en el dormitorio
agonizaba la hermana, a solas, escuchando
el ruido de la cuchara en el plato, del tenedor
en la carne y el silencio de mi abuelo.
Después del funeral
y del decoro respectivo, vino la guerra
y mi abuelo que se iba con los ojos cerrados
en un carro de tercera.
Demasiadas personas opinaron flagrantes en contra
de sus 18 años, palabras plenas de pacifismo
y lógicamente engarzadas hacia un bien común familiar:
en primer lugar las del padrastro,
consecuentes todas con la justicia, etc.
Vitry, Verdún, Aix-la-Chapelle, Versalles en 1919
y regresó para conocer a mí abuela:
mi abuela tuvo a mi madre, mi madre me tuvo a mí.
Yo comencé a esperar sentado a que me llamasen, luego
me puse de pie, ahora
voy hacia allá pero no encuentro a nadie.

Backsliding

In my house there were few fortunate scenes.
My grandfather had just turned eighteen
and a stepfather showed up who sat
at the head of the table; in the bedroom
his sister was dying, alone, listening
to the sound of the spoon on the plate, of the fork
in the meat and my grandfather's silence.
After the funeral
and the respectful decorum, the war came
and my grandfather was going away with his eyes closed
in a third-class train car.
Too many people were dead set against
his going at eighteen, using words full of pacifism
logically strung together in favor of a familiar common good:
in first place the stepfather's,
all of them consistent with justice, etc.
Vitry, Verdun, Aix-la-Chapelle, Versailles in 1919
and he returned to meet my grandmother:
my grandmother had my mother, my mother had me.
I began to wait till they called me, later
I got up, now
I'm coming but don't find anyone.

Las presas son

Se rompe el huevo y sale el pollo dando píos
de infinita imbecilidad, tambaleándose por el nido,
hasta decidirse a decir mamá.
Mamá, dónde estás? Tengo frío. Tengo hambre.
Y se fue bamboleando las plumas tiesas, buscándola.
Mamá, dónde estás?
Alguien contó la historia al almuerzo.
Se rieron todos. Se rieron mucho.
Me reí yo, con la cazuela en la boca y pregunté:
la mamá, dónde está?

The Chicken Pieces Are

The egg is broken and the chick comes out cheeping
with an infinite imbecility, staggering through the nest,
until it decides to say mother.
Mother, where are you? I'm cold. I'm hungry.
And it went tottering on its stiff feathers, hunting her.
Mother, where are you?
Someone told the story at lunch.
Everybody laughed. They laughed a lot.
I laughed, asked with the drumstick in my mouth:
The mother, where is she?

La muerte en boca de alguien

La extraviada fotografía familiar
apareció entre las cosas de la Nana, tres días
después del entierro. Figuraban todos
en el patio de la casa, de pie o sentados,
en torno a los abuelos. La madre
no miraba de frente, quizá buscando al padre
más que nunca esa tarde. Era como si
algo los hubiera reunido para fijarlos por siempre
con esa actitud de buena familia a la luz
del sol. Los hermanos, con una ajena seriedad
en el cuerpo, observaban el suelo con las manos rígidas
y no obstante yo sonreía al fotógrafo, junto
a la Nana y a una mata de gladiolos que ya no existe.
Tuviéramos que reunirnos de nuevo de esa manera
alguna tarde en estos años, nos encontraríamos con más
de un cadáver peinándose para la pose.

Death in Someone's Mouth

The mislaid family photograph
turned up among the Nanny's things, three days
after the interment. It pictured everyone
in the backyard, standing or seated,
surrounding the grandparents. Mother
wasn't looking straight ahead, perhaps searching for dad
more than ever that afternoon. It was as if
something had reunited them to fix them forever
with that attitude of a good family in the light
of the sun. The brothers, with a strange seriousness
to their bodies, stared at the ground with rigid hands
and nevertheless I smiled at the photographer, next
to the Nanny and a patch of gladiolas that no longer exist.
These days if we had to gather again in that way
some afternoon, we would find ourselves with more
than one corpse combing itself for the camera.

III

La manzana del gusano

III

The Worm's Apple

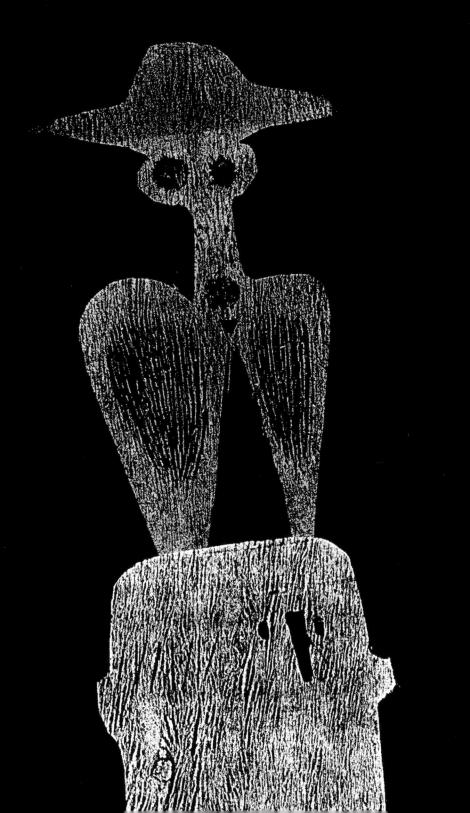

Bitácora

Amo la coronta de la manzana comida por ti,
dejada en el cenicero, entre mis colillas,
con sus pepas y tallo olvidados,
como para que yo simplemente los mire
y recuerde que donde ahora estás no es lejos,
pero que nunca conoceré el camino.

Binnacle

I love the apple core you ate down to,
stuck in the ashtray, with my cigarette butts,
its seeds and stems left behind
simply so I may look at them
and remember that where you are isn't far,
though I'll never know the way.

Autobiografía

Toda la vida me la he pasado
enviando telegramas
a causa principalmente de
citas insuficientes
deseos de reencuentro
necesidad de saber de ti
noches de insomnio y las más
de locura gravitando
en torno a tu presencia
siempre viajera pero
no eres culpable ni
yo lo soy
así es que sigamos en lo mismo:
huyendo
y persiguiéndonos con palabras.

Autobiography

All my life I have spent
sending telegrams
mainly because of
not enough meetings
wanting to get together again
the need to hear from you
sleepless nights and mostly
a madness gravitating
toward your presence
ever on the move but
you are not to blame nor
am I
so this is why we'll go on the same:
running away
and after one another with words.

Sacrificio

Traeré el vino para humedecer
esta fiesta de tu boca
con mi boca en tu ombligo y tu vientre;
nada ha de permanecer
no humedecido
ahora que los dioses
han desechado la sangre mía
por la leche de tus senos.

Sacrifice

I'll bring the wine for moistening
this feast of your mouth
with my mouth on your navel and abdomen;
nothing will remain
unmoistened
now that the gods
have rejected my blood
for the milk of your breasts.

Aquelarre

Asaz poderoso el nervio formidable de tu ojo
escudriña el flanco desnudo de mi cuerpo que ostenta
el músculo sexual enrollado cual cinturón.
Tu mano se extiende y agarra la fruta de mi ingle
que exangüe pende en un exceso de desnudez.
Atribuyo tu gesto al amor desatado, al deseo que invade
esta hora de calma, provista ella toda
de las necesarias modulaciones provenientes del silencio.
Tu llamamiento es lupino: acudo a la carnada
tendida de tus senos y arrojo mi hocico
como gubia dislocada en tu blandura feroz.

Witches' Sabbath

So powerful the enormous optic nerve of your eye
that scrutinizes the nude side of my body as it displays
the sexual muscle cylindrical as any belt.
Your hand reaches out and grasps the fruit of my groin
that hangs exhausted in an excess nakedness.
I attribute your gesture to a ferocity of love, the desire that invades
this hour of calm, provided with all
the necessary modulations resulting from silence.
Your call is wolfish: I answer to the extended
enticement of your breasts and thrust my snout
like a disjointed chisel into your ferocious softness.

Justina velocísima

Buenas noches, Justina,
hoy he venido a verte así es que déjame
entrar para decirte que sé que estás sola
y tanto tú como yo lo deseamos
este amor con el que te desnudo
y ahora poseo
sobre la alfombra del hall
porque no ha habido tiempo
para pasarme a tu cama
u ocasión para decirte de otra manera
te amo
y hacer entonces lo mismo que hacemos ahora.

So Quickly Justine

Good evening, Justine,
I have come to see you so let me
in to tell you that I know that you're alone
and that you as much as I desire it
this love with which I undress and
now possess you
on the hall carpet
because there hasn't been time
to make it to your bed
or to say to you in any other way
I love you
and to do what now we do.

La forma más rugosa del amor

Resto soy de una terrible masturbación
que realicé a propósito de algo que no recuerdo
y quise entonces vaciarme enteramente
sobre cualquier cosa, piso
cama o pantalón, me daba lo mismo.
Prolongué mi acto más y más,
lo más que pude y comencé a recordar
tantas cosas de otro tiempo:
que no voy a enumerar aquí ni en ninguna
otra parte, pues me estoy masturbando nuevamente
y ya sube
de no sé dónde de mi fondo adentro
esta amargura.

The Coarsest Form of Love

Reduced I am by a terrible masturbation
that I performed for some reason I can't recall
and I wanted then to empty myself entirely
on whatever, floor
bed or pants, it didn't matter.
I prolonged my act more and more,
as long as I could and began to remember
so many things from another time:
that I am not going to enumerate here or
anywhere else, because I am doing it again
and already is arising from
I don't know where deep inside me
this bitter grief.

Los 28 días del árbol

Siento tu fondo todo entero vivo y menstruando,
en silencio mascando mi carne
y arriba te muerdo los ojos, cogote, boca y demás,
como si en esta oscuridad fuera permisible
mi erótica servidumbre. Vamos
en busca de la guagua innominada, dormida
y no nuestra, todavía pensamiento, por hoy pensamiento,
la guagua-consuelo que fluye en la sangre
de la cópula nuestra, tu sagrada menstruación
consumando el engaño:
todo es destituir, o quizá retener; mi marca obstinada
te obsequia el resuello, la restregadura
de mis partes fijas en ti y en ti. Simuladamente
digo un nombre pequeño, apto
para un ser pequeño, y acabo boca arriba a tu lado
lo que boca abajo comencé tan en silencio.

The 28 Days of the Tree

I feel your total depths entirely alive and menstruating,
in silence chewing my flesh
and above I bite your eyes, neck, mouth and the rest,
as if in this darkness my erotic servitude
were permitted. We go
in search of the unnamed child, asleep
and not ours, still a thought, for today a thought,
the child-consolement flowing in the blood
of our copulation, your sacred menstruation
consuming the deception:
all is to destroy, or perhaps to retain; my obstinate mark
bestows your panting, the rubbing
of my firm parts in you and in you. Feigningly
I say a little name, apt
for a little being, and I finish face up at your side
what I began face down in such silence.

El dorso de la mano

Me das y yo te cojo en movimiento,
redondas, suaves, balanceándose como un columpio
blanco, todo lleno de misterio, en tanto
que la partidura se convierte en un ángulo profundo
y yo comienzo a cavar mi sueño.

The Back of the Hand

You offer me and I take you in motion,
round, soft, rocking side to side as on a white
swing, completely filled with mystery, so much so
that your steep cliff develops into a deep angle
and I begin to dig my dream.

Las intenciones

Estas ahí de pie atendiendo tus cosas
y me das la espalda absorta en tus cosméticos:
mi mano encuentra tu seno suave
y desesperado intento llegar hasta tu centro
a través del prolén de tu falda que me resiste
hasta el momento de mi derrame
en mi propia bragueta y yo quedo húmedo
temblando de frío y tú quedas
sonriendo excitada con mi pequeña muerte
y le lanzas un beso al espejo que yo recibo de rebote
y me enfrentas
y vienes hacia mí tan lentamente apagando la luz.

The Intentions

You are there standing attending to your things
and with your back to me absorbed in your make-up:
my hand finds your soft breast
and desperately I try to reach your center
through the back of your skirt that you resist
till I have wet
my fly and I remain damp
trembling with cold and you keep
smiling excited by my small death
and you throw a kiss at the mirror that I receive indirectly
and you face me
and come toward me so slowly turning off the light.

El apóstata

Te lo llevaste, yo estaba de acuerdo,
a una casa de sombras,
a una camilla blanca que no conozco,
yo estaba de acuerdo, y la anestesia te dijo:
volveré sola, sí yo estaba de acuerdo,
y te dormiste mirando tus zapatos debajo de la silla.

The Apostate

You yourself took him, I agreed,
to a house of shadows,
to a small white surgical table I do not know,
I was in agreement, and the anesthesia told you:
I will return alone, yes I agreed
and you fell asleep looking at your shoes beneath the chair.

Me hubiera gustado quedarme aquí

Una canción de boda compuesta de aire inmóvil,
de tierra seca, para darte una nueva dimensión
de amor, deposito en un embudo de papel
por la cerradura de la puerta de tu casa, mientras
me vuelvo viejo regresando a mi polvo y a mi noche.

I Would Have Liked to Have Stayed Here

A wedding song composed of unmoving air,
of dry earth, for giving you a new dimension
of love, I deposit in a roll of paper
through the keyhole of the door of your home, as
I grow old returning to my dust and to my night.

oliverwelden@gmail.com